Noisy toys

Ann Langran and Mark Nutting

This book will help you to find out about toys that make a noise. Some of the toys make music and some make noises just for fun.

You do not have to read this book from beginning to end. Just turn to the pages that interest you.

Contents

Why are some toys noisy?

Noisy toys are fun.

Noise makes many toys more interesting.

Some toys would be useless if they did not make a noise.

The noise in this rattle is made with beads.

There are different ways of getting toys to make sounds.

You shake a rattle.
You strike a xylophone.
You press a squeaky toy.
You blow a whistle.
You ring a bell.

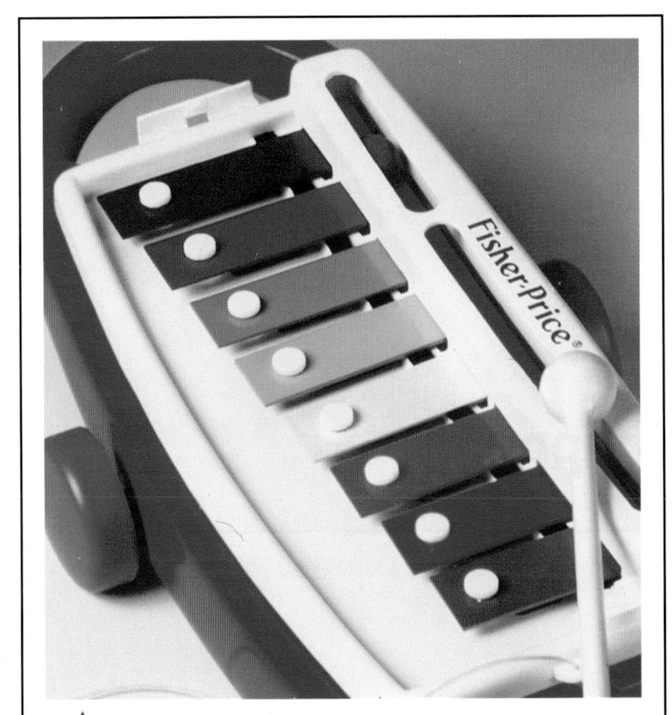

This xylophone would be boring if it did not make a sound.

You turn the knob to make a sound.

Toys for babies

Many baby toys make sounds.
Babies love these noisy toys.

They help to keep babies happy.

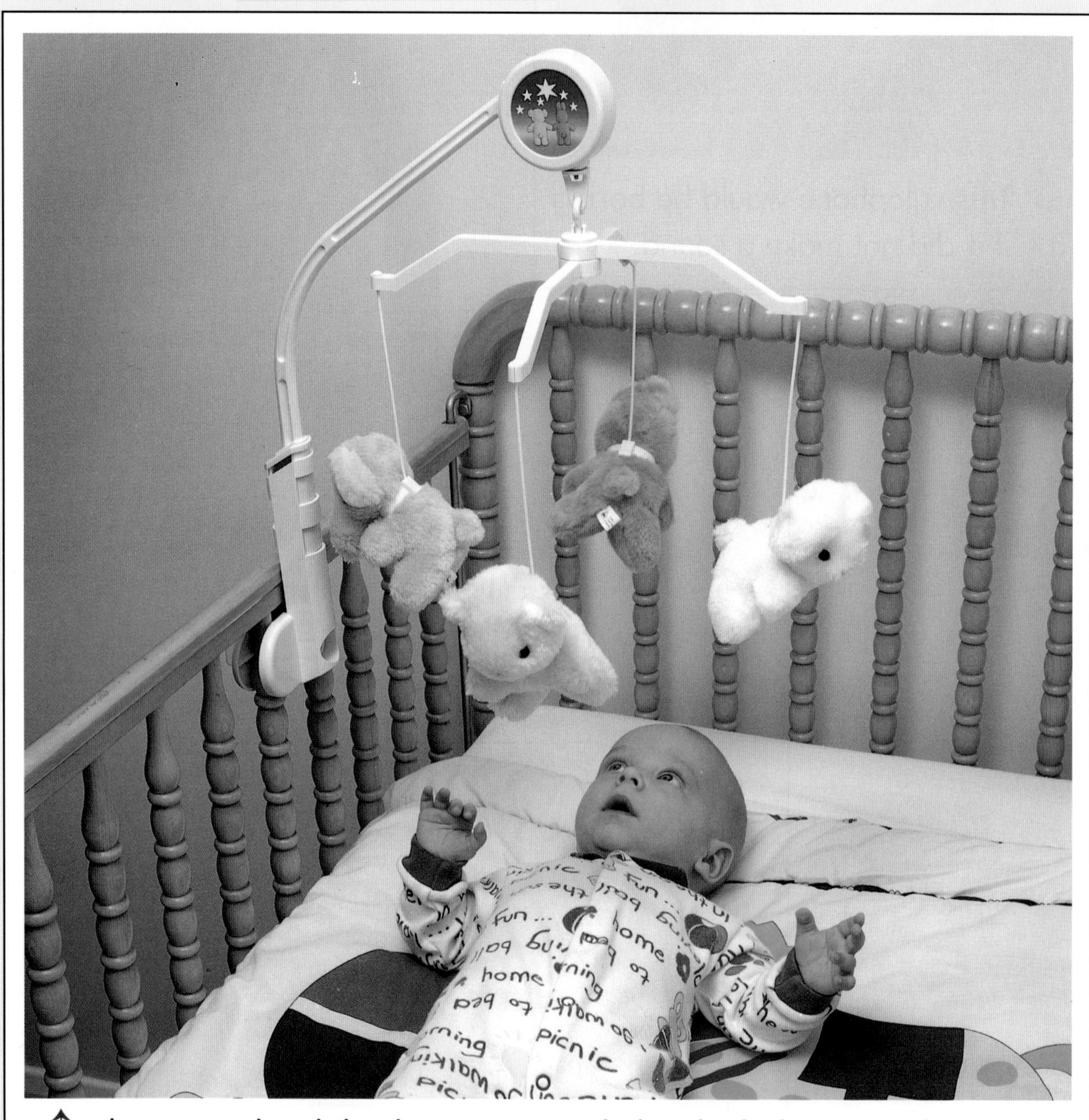

This musical mobile plays a tune. It helps the baby go to sleep.

Grown-ups often show babies how to work the noisy toys. Then babies learn how to make the toys noisy for themselves. They keep on making the noise.

Some grown-ups wish the babies would stop playing with the toys.

Babies quickly learn how to get this toy to make different noises.

Small children love pulling toys that make a noise.

Musical toys

Most children enjoy music.
There are two sorts of musical toys.

1. Musical toys that you play yourself.

2. Toys that play music for you to listen to.

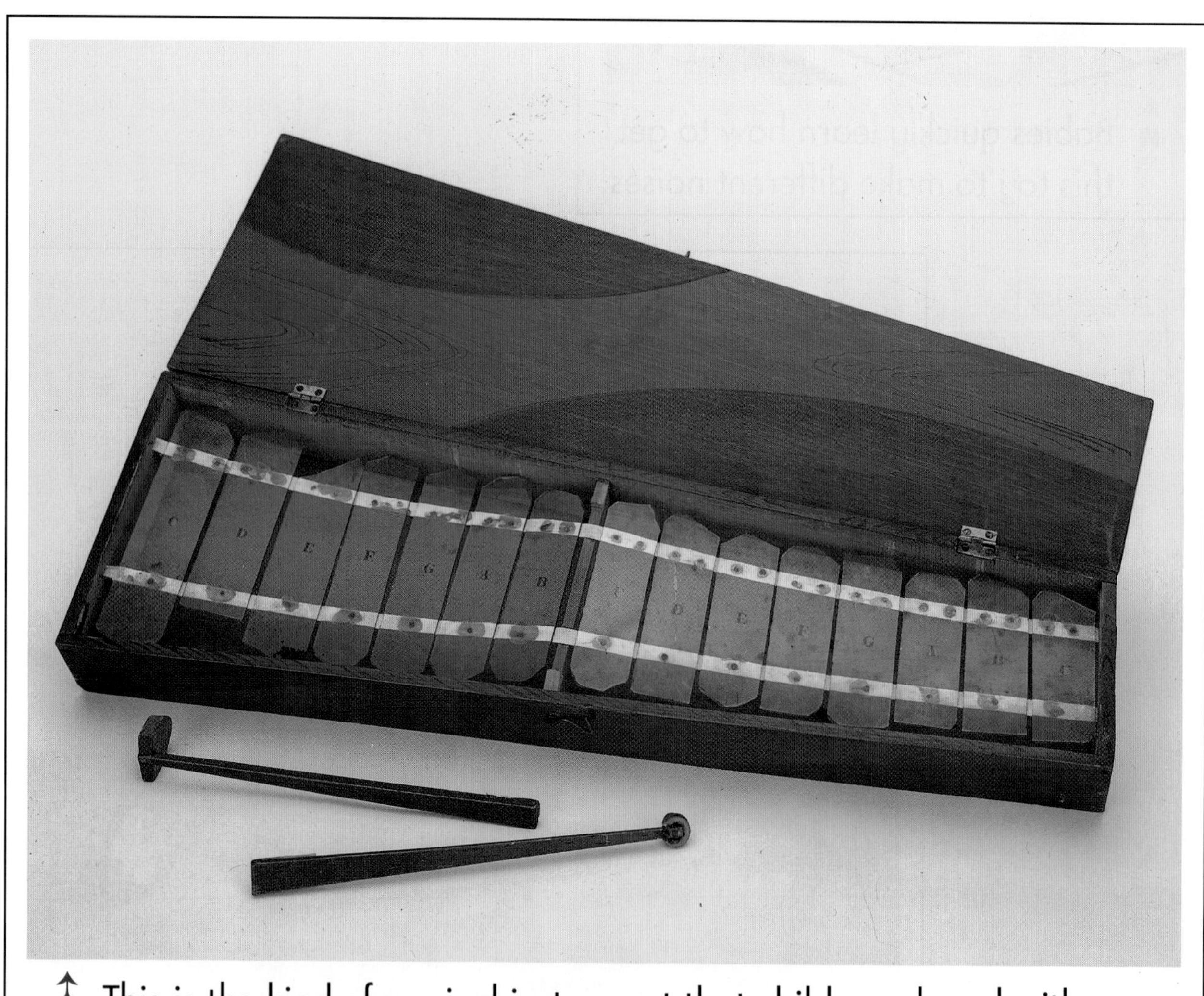

↑ This is the kind of musical instrument that children played with a hundred years ago.

Many musical toys are copies of real musical instruments.
To make the music they are played in different ways.

You strum a guitar.

You blow a trumpet.

You bang a drum.

You press the keys on a keyboard.

More musical toys

**There are many toys that play music for children to listen to.
Children have always loved to play with toys that look like the real thing.**

Record players for grown-ups were first made in 1887. The record player in the photograph was made for children in 1925. It works when you turn the handle.

Cassette recorders were first made in 1963.
Children use them to listen to music and stories.
This cassette recorder needs batteries to make it work.

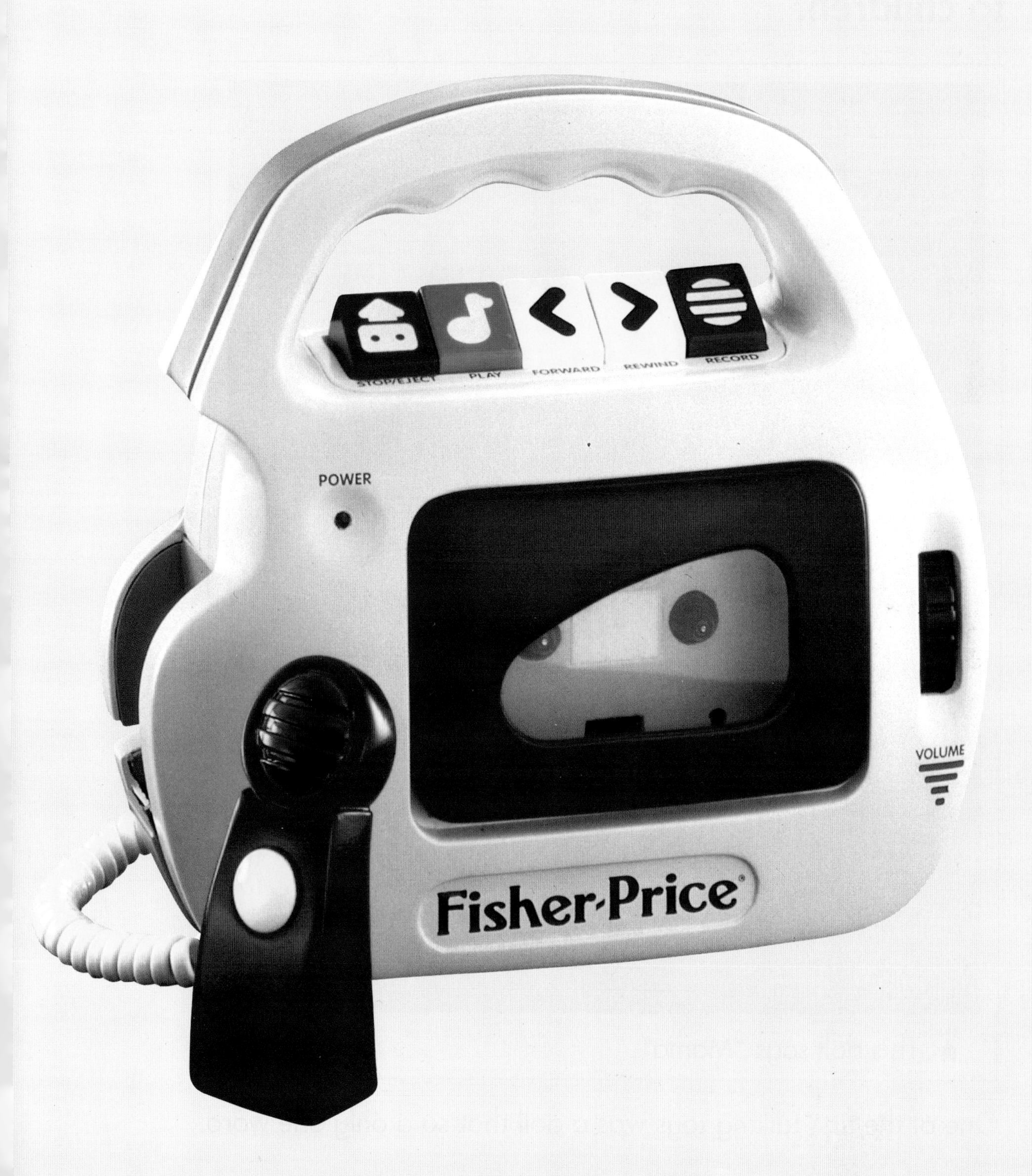

Talking toys

**Children like talking to toys.
There are some toys that can talk back to children.**

This doll says "Mama".

One of the first talking toys was a doll that said only one word.

Talking dolls made about twenty years ago could say more than one word.

Now there are toys that listen to you and follow instructions.

When you pull a string this toy can say five different things.

This talking toy can say a lot of things. It can ask questions.

Electronic toys

Lots of toy cars and fluffy animals do not make any noise, but some do. The toys shown here make a noise. They are electronic.

The dog barks when it is switched on.

Children enjoy these electronic noises.
They make the toys seem more like the real thing.
Some grown-ups do not like the noises.

These toys need batteries to make siren sounds.

The truck makes noises and moves when you talk to it.

Noisy games

Games can be very noisy.

These games make noises when they are played. The people playing the games make noises too.

This game makes a buzzing noise.

This game sounds like a sea battle.

When the games are played the same noises are heard again and again. This can upset people who are not playing the game, but most children think noisy games and toys are fun.

Many electronic games sound the same.

Glossary of words used in this book

Battery	A battery is a power box. It makes electricity. You put batteries inside some toys to make them work.
Electronic	Electronic toys have small computer chips and bits inside them. Electricity and batteries make them work.
Keyboard	A keyboard is a musical instrument which has white and black keys like a piano. The sound is made by pressing the keys with your fingers.
Musical mobile	A mobile is a hanging toy that moves. A musical mobile plays a tune.
Siren	A siren is a machine which makes a loud noise. The noise warns people about something. Fire engines, police cars and ambulances use sirens.
Xylophone	A xylophone is a musical instrument made of flat bars of wood or metal. You play it by hitting the bars with small hammers.